821.914   Mozz.
MOZ

    In search of the
    holey whale.

$17.95   000048007
               02/15/2010

DATE			

IN SEARCH OF

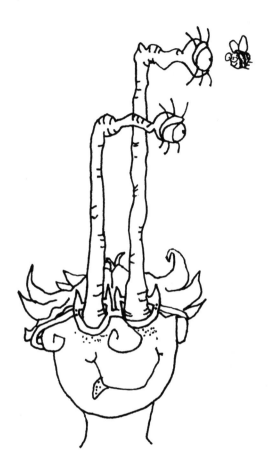

THE HOLEY WHALE

Goofy Guru Publishing presents . . .

IN SEARCH OF
THE HOLEY WHALE
The Top Secret Riddles &
Left-Handed Scribbles

of

Mozzzzz...

Goofy Guru Publishing
Alice Apple, Editor-in-Chief
405 Kiowa Place, Boulder, CO 80303, USA
goofygurupress@comcast.net
www.goofyguru.com

Design by Jane Raese

Arigatoh-oh t' Silvine, the Silver Sage,
for her enriching rhyme & rhythm recipes,
t' Lady Lyngo-go f' those darlin' dots & dashes,
and t' Alpha Ali-oop, the most beautiful blob in the cosmos.

Library of Congress Control Number: 2007941967
ISBN 0-9726130-3-X

Printed in China
First printing

For
Tommy
Purr

IN SEARCH OF THE HOLEY WHALE

(The Key to the Kingdumb of Utter Mozzsense)

I've sailed the Sea of Where and Why
In hopes that I might some day spy
The sacred Holey Whale,
Riddled with a hundred holes—
The mightiest of salty souls
From splashing spout to tail.

For Holey holds the key alone
To open up the Great Unknown,
Unlock all cloudy things.
And there within its whaley presence,
One soon will know the very essence
Of mozzsense—whence it springs.

I've cruised the endless sloppy green,
And wide-eyed wonders I have seen—
The Shoals of Curious Cod,
The Senseless Seal, the Schools of Doubt,
The Walrus Tryin' to Work Things Out,
And lots that's very odd.

I've seen red herrings by the score,
Merry Mackerels near the shore,
Many a Guppy of Grief.
The fate of swordfish after duels,
The flounders who become life's fools,
And sharks beyond belief.

But sadly of the Holey Whale
I've never yet seen fin nor tail
Upon time's fishing line.
But one day soon on the bouncing brine,
Holey will appear like a mystic sign,
And in that very moment . . . all mozzsense will be mine!

So all aboard, sail on, sail on!
Till the Holey Whale it comes along,

And then, and then, and then . . .

There'll be a splash, a blinding flash,
A taily flip, a splish, a splat,

And all will be mozzsense

After that.

8

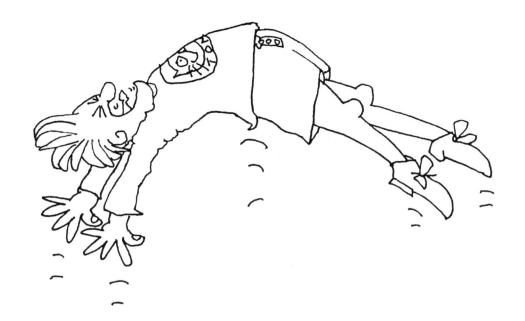

THE PRICKLES OF PLEASURE

I've sat in beds of buttercups,
I've lain in daisies too.
I've stretched right out in fields of poppies,
I've rolled in bells of blue.
I've looked up at the cloudless skies,
And felt the urge to whistle.
But then I've spoiled it all somehOOOW
By sitting on a thistle!

LET ME INTRODUCE MY RELATIVES TO YOU
(*An Excuse for the Things I Do*)

My uncle, The Messy Muncher,
Was an awfully uncultured vulture
From an off-shoot family line,
Who always arrived for dinner
Just after we'd wined and dined.
He'd sit there on the table
(His manners were terribly rude)
And grovel and generally gorge himself
Among the scraps of food.

My aunt, The Great Plate Cleaner,
A ravenous wild hyena,
Was nearly just as bad.
She'd scavenge through the slops,
Which made my parents mad.
She'd lick the dishes sparkling clean—
No thought of knife or fork—
Then give a growl, a hound dog howl, .
Which passed for table talk.

So if, by chance, you're upset by
The way I use my nose
For eating peas, or taste ice cream
By dipping in my toes,
Or knit spaghetti, or juggle sprouts
(Each meal's a circus show),
Then blame those messy so-and-so's.
I copied them, you know.

GROWING UP NATURALLY

Like a tiny seed
My mother waters me.
(She wants her son, you see,
To grow up naturally.)
And as she tucks me into bed,
And down I lay my sleepy head,
I know I'm growing more and more
With every passing hour,
For now, instead of "Buddy"
She calls me "Little Flower."

13

THE GREAT BOARD SWALLOWER

Mister Jaws explored
His stomach's floor
By daringly swallowing boards—
Long three-by-fours (nails and all),
A table leg, and half a door—
A trick the audience adored.
And then when his stomach could take no more,
Mister Jaws simply swallowed a saw.

COMPLETE CONFIDENCE
IN YOUR APP "EAR" ANCE

Embarrassed by bald ears?
Don't be, help is near.

Now earwigs are here,
The fashion "Hit of the Year."

Never again will you have to hide your head,
Ashamed, blushing, turning red.

Never again will you shed those silent tears,
Sadly thinking, "If only I didn't have such bald ears."

So go on, drown your worries, your fears,
Hip, hip, hurrah, and add three cheers—

Earwigs are here!

WHERE ARE YOU, CAPTAIN ETERNITY?
(*Or What's in a Name?*)

Oh Captain Eternity,
The big, the brave, the terribly strong,
The fearless fighter of right against wrong—
Oh Captain Eternity, come on,
Please don't be long.

There's a goldfish that's about to drown,
There's a sunny-side egg turned upside down,
There's lots of lost luggage still to be found!
Oh Captain Eternity,
Why aren't you around?

There's a knife that's threatening a sweet bread roll,
There's a shoe that's searching for its sole.
There's a slice of cheese being attacked by mold!
Oh Captain Eternity,
Weren't you told?

There's a sea out there getting soaking wet,
There's a hole that's caught in a great big net,
There's a poor hot dog in need of a vet!
Oh Captain Eternity,
How come you're not here yet?

As the sun sets,
As time trickles by,
As the minutes turn into hours,
As we wait for your strength, your amazing powers—
Oh Captain Eternity, come on,
Oh *please* don't be long!

BATHING BEAUTY

Egyptian archeologists insist at last
They've unearthed that relic of the past—Cleopatra's bath.
(The one she filled with gallons of milk
To keep her skin as smooth as silk.)

What's more, they say they've discovered a straw
Lying by the side of it,
And although they'd prefer not to think of it,
Questions arise among the wise,
Did the queen (now here's a beauty tip)
In that milk not only sit
But sometimes take a little sip?

THE SOAP OPERA OF LIFE

To sum up the life of a bar of soap:
Diligence, duty, hard work, hope.
A madcap mission to keep us clean—
Postman, plumber, tycoon, queen—
Behind our ears, between our toes
(Sarah's, Billy's, Wendy's, Joe's).

But what does it get for all its troubles—
Nothing but a great big mouthful of bubbles!

SENSATIONAL SCISSORS

Mister Snippit, the hairdresser,
Around the town is known
For marvelous modern creations
With scissors, brush, and comb.

But still I suppose he's better known
For what he dares to wear,
Believing a real hairdresser
Should always dress in . . . hair!

MEOWING MAT

The Flat Cat's small and squat,
But round and overweight it's not.
Instead—an ironing board with paws,
A welcome mat with tail and claws.

The good point with this flattened breed,
A cat-flap's not a thing you'll need.
It simply runs along the floor
And slides beneath the door.

SURVIVAL OF THE KNITTEST

The Woolly Mammoth,
It is no more,
And that's because
(I'm pretty sure)
In Ice Age times
They liked to sit
And quietly knit
Long scarves from it.

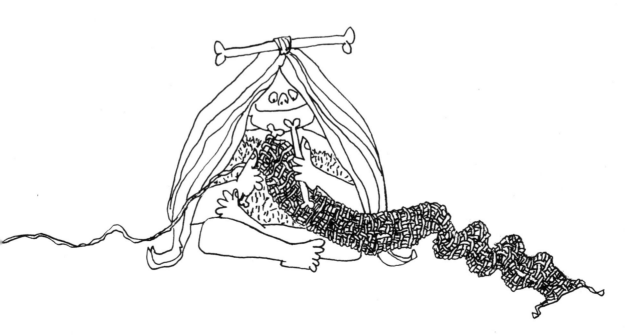

HERMIT CRAB HAT

The latest seaside fashion line
Is the "hermit crab design."
A hat where you can go and hide
If feeling rather shy,
A place to disappear inside
And wave the world goodbye.

FOLDED FLIGHT

His plan
Was to be the first man
To fly around the world in a paper plane,
But sadly . . . it rained!

(Though now he's getting set
To try again . . . in a cardboard jet!)

THE TROJAN PIG

I suppose by now, of course,
You've heard of the Trojan Horse?
Though far less known, but just as big,
Was the wooden Trojan Pig.

Outside of Troy they left that thing,
But no one dared to bring it in.
Not from fear but rather, well—
Much much worse than the fires of Hell—
That awful, revolting . . .

Piggy smell!

PS:
I bet you're thinking—
But what of those all stuffed inside?
It can't have been a bed of roses,
Still there they sat all safe and snug,
With clothespins on their noses.

27

SHOCKING SHOOTS

Oh pity the poor pandas,
With not a second's peace
At mealtimes in their leafy groves—
Their worries never cease.

They're always in a state of shock,
From sunrise to sunset,
Their stomachs tied in lots of knots,
They're nervous wrecks I bet.

For when,
Again 'n' again 'n' again,

They chew their bam**BOO!**

Well . . . you'd be nervous too.

ROOSTER WRISTWATCH

The Rooster Wristwatch is perfect
For telling the time at dawn,
You don't have to wind it up,
It merely runs on corn.
There's a ready built-in alarm
For that early morning call,
Though at telling the time in the afternoon
It's not so good at all.
In fact, I'm thinking of taking it back
To that "All Organic Shop,"
For every night about eight o'clock . . .
It always seems to stop!

ANOTHER NICE DAY
(In the Life of Little Sunny Ray)

"Have a really, really, really nice day,"
Said the sweet salesgirl to Sunny Ray
As he left the Cosmic Cookie Store
And ran WHAM into the half-closed door.
That is, before the sky grew thick and dark
And began to meow, moo, and bark.
For, yes, it rained *real* cats and dogs,
A puzzled cow, raccoons and frogs,
Whose din drowned out the terrible roar
Now pouring from a lion's jaws—
The one gone missing from the zoo
That chased him spitting poisonous glue.
(A breed of lion completely new!)
But stepping on some upturned rakes,
He fell into a pit of snakes
And crawled among that squirming mess
Till down a vulture swooped, no less,
And grabbed him firmly by the wrist
And flew him up through mountain mist,
Where vulturettes, all mild and meek,
Did open up their razor beaks
And would have eaten him up whole
If not for that wild wind so cold
That numbed that big bird's vicelike grip,
And down he fell toward a ship
That drifted on a soggy sea,
The color of Darjeeling tea.

But—phew!—he didn't hit the deck
Of Captain Cod, ol' Barnacle Neck,
But landed in the ocean—SPLASH—
And found himself all bound and lashed
By tentacles of Squirmy Sid,
That one and only dancing squid,
Who then began a jovial jig
All dressed up in a seaweed wig,
Till Sunny found himself ignored,
Washed up on some far unknown shore
A million miles from his own door.

So up he crawled that endless beach
Where plum trees grew that smelled of peach,
And killer crabs there snapped and nipped
Till all his clothes were torn and ripped,
And space-sick Zonglies cruised the skies
With three left ears and wonky eyes,
And waving armchairs watched the fun
Beneath a blackened rotting sun.
And as he crawled up that strange shore,
He met five cannibals, maybe more,
Who lived by one quite simple law—
They never ate their victims raw.
And so they tied him 'tween two poles
'N' pinched 'n' poked 'n' tweaked his soles.
And through that land they carried him
Toward the world's most distant rim,
And there they cooked a pot of broth
All covered in a smelly froth.

But, ah, before they could tuck in
There came a witch (the salesgirl's twin),
Who changed that pot to What Was Not.
And there he was in a small cot,
And life began when he was born
With morning light from the First Dawn
That spread across the seven skies,
Till gosh, to his extreme surprise,
All guided by the Hand of Fate
He found himself at his own gate.
And as he rose and stretched his limbs,
His mother stood in front of him
And sweetly asked, quite naturally
(As any mom would do, you see),
"Oh Sunny Ray, did you have a nice day?"
Well . . . what in the world could he say?

MUD PIES AND FRIES

I'm feeling rather yucky
(You say that's no surprise),
I think my stomach's bigger,
Much bigger than my eyes.

'Cause from the playground kitchen
I ordered two mud pies,
A plate of twigs and lollipop sticks
That tasted just like fries.

I know that I was greedy
To eat not one, but two.
Perhaps I should have had instead
That dish of sandpit stew!

PUNCTURED PLANT

And now to speak of the garden leek,
A veggie quite unique,
A plant that has a puncture so . . .
In spring it springs a leak!

Just open up your mouth,
Take one, pop it in.
Immediately the stuff within,

    Dribbles

          down

      your

        chin!

TENNIS ANYONE?

Who's for tennis in Cobra Court?
Hide and seek in Werewolf Wood?
Who's for climbing Hippo Hill?
The exercise will do you good!

Who's for tag in Grizzly Grove?
A swim in South Shark Sea?
Picnicking in Panther Park?
What? No one coming, only me?

Come on, come on, it's a lovely day—
Okay . . . how about a walk down Bee Sting Way?

THE BAT BOYS

All day long the Bat Boys
Simply hang around,
Coming out at night
To cruise the sleeping ground.

They flap their waxy wings,
Speak supersonic slang,
Every one a member of
The Big Nocturnal Gang.

Swooping through the streets,
Nightmares in the air,
Bombing screaming girls,
Whistling past their hair.

With fangy smiles they are
The Kings of Graveyard Way,
Till come the first sun's rays, and they
Hang out another day.

MOLDY OL' MOON

If ever you pay the moon a visit,
Never sit on it.
For if you do then very soon
You'll start a-scratching and a-squirming,
Your skin will start a-burning,
And then you'll have an itching fit—
One that'll never quit.
So please just walk (but rather quickly)—
Don't sit down on it!
It's sure to make you sickly—
An illness hard to fix,
For after all, that moldy moon
Is full of lunar ticks!

OL' SUGAR TONGUE

Oh, oh, oh, the crow
Has the sweetest voice of any bird
I'm sure you've ever heard.
Its song so divine, so sublime,
So serene to listeners' ears—
A mesmerizing masterpiece
That brings them all to tears.
A sparkling stream where every note
Pours out like starlight from its throat.
Oh, a singer of such charm and grace, such lovely melodies,
It's simply named "Ol' Sugar Tongue, the Syrup of the Trees."
But, oh, I suppose, all this you know—
That is, of course . . . if you're a crow!

HAPPY RETURNS OF THE DAY

The Pigyou (rather than the Pygmy) Tribe
Deep in their jungle home,
Use the banana boomerang
As through the trees they roam.
And though I'm relieved to say
They rarely hit a thing this way,
At least at the end of the day,
With this kind of hunting
They're always able
To munch on something!

RHINOCERUST

From several miles away
You'll hear a clang, a clank!
Oh here it comes, that pile of junk,
The Great Safari Tank—
An armor-plated overcoat;
A dust ball for a brain;
A creaking, squeaking, rusting wreck
From standing in the rain.

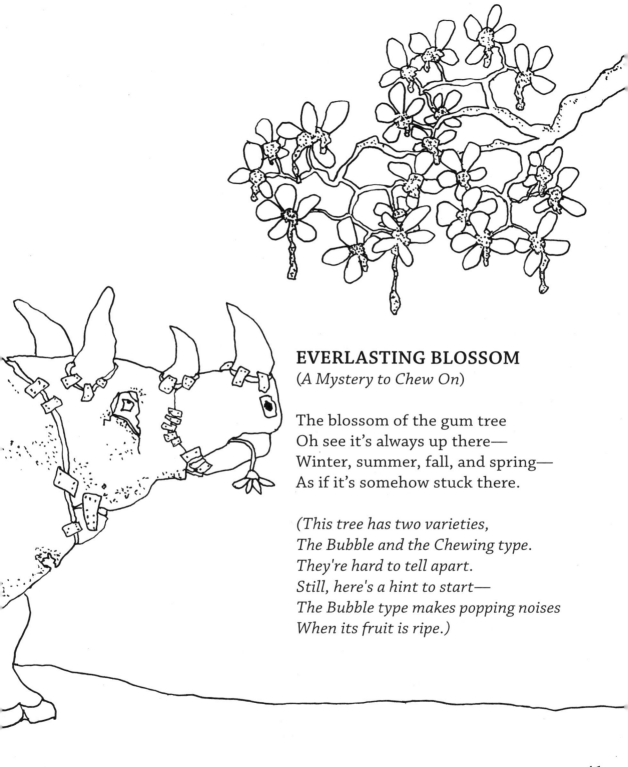

EVERLASTING BLOSSOM
(*A Mystery to Chew On*)

The blossom of the gum tree
Oh see it's always up there—
Winter, summer, fall, and spring—
As if it's somehow stuck there.

(*This tree has two varieties,*
The Bubble and the Chewing type.
They're hard to tell apart.
Still, here's a hint to start—
The Bubble type makes popping noises
When its fruit is ripe.)

PUMPED-UP PIANO

The blow-up piano
Is really neat
For picnics, parties—
A musical treat.

For if by chance
Someone bursts into song,
You can blow up the piano
And play along.

THE PROMISE

I promise to be good,
I promise to be fair,
I promise I'll not lie,
I promise I will share.

I promise to clean my room,
I promise to make my bed,
I promise to . . . er . . . sometimes
Take back what I just said!

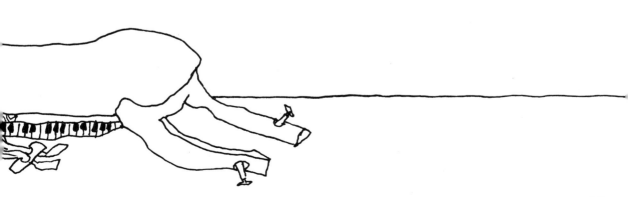

CIRCUS SOCKS

I own a pair of nice striped socks,
The nicest pair you'll ever meet.
And if they're worn for several weeks,
They walk without my feet!

Day by day I trained them both
To leap through hoops and over boots,
To walk the clothesline in the yard—
No net or parachutes.

Then to the circus, off they went,
My "Twin Performing Socks,"
And people swarmed to that big top—
They lined a hundred blocks.

Parents, children filled that tent,
Excitement filled the air,
And when my clever socks appeared,
I said a little prayer.

They tiptoed 'cross the tightrope
Up there at dizzy heights,
And I was very proud of them—
Their names spelled out in lights!

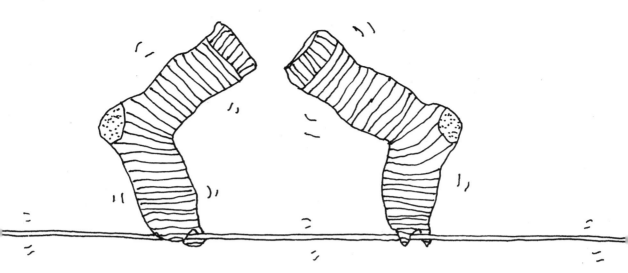

But then the awful happened.
One sock looked 'round, then tripped . . .
That caused its friend to wobble
And both to lose their grip.

And down 'n' down 'n' down they fell,
Right in the audience—PLOP!
In minutes then, confusion reigned . . .
The screaming wouldn't stop.

PHEEEEEEEW! PHEEEEEEEW! PHEEEEEEEW!
All gasped and held their noses,
But what was all the fuss about?
Socks don't smell like roses!

Then from that tent the audience ran,
As if it were on fire,
Not running from a pair of socks
Just fallen from a wire.

And roared the Great Ringmaster,
"GET OUT, AND DON'T COME BACK!"
Though to this day I can't see why
I had to have the sack.

Oh what a dreadful day that was—
A day I'll not forget.
My socks just sat and sniffed and sobbed—
Their wool was sopping wet.

But patiently I stroked their stripes,
"Don't worry, it's okay,"
And put them back upon my feet.
That's where they are today!

And to those socks an oath I swore,
I promised there and then,
I'd never, *ever*, **ever, EVER**
Take them off again!

AUNT ENNA

*(Another relative of mine—one who
always gets a good reception in our house)*

Tall and thin Aunt Enna
Makes a great antenna,
Especially when she comes for tea
And stands on our TV.

SPEEDING ON SWAN LAKE

The rarely seen
High-speed breed,
The Supersonic Swan,
Upon the lake goes sailing on
Twice as fast as other fellas—
The only one to evolve propellers.

ONE-LEGGED LOONEY

Observe the heron, the ibis,
Tall and rather gawkish,
Who balance cleverly on one leg
While eyeballing the fish.
But here's the Befuddled Flamingo
With plumage sunset red
That somehow likes instead
To stand upon its head.
Of course old ways can't be denied,
So naturally that's why,
Within those wet and weedy depths
Instincts never die.
For though it stands upon its head,
It raises just one leg.
(And nobody knows for sure
How it lays an egg!)

The Aquatic Adventures of
CAPTAIN BOOK AND HIS CREW
OF RAGGED READERS

The not-so-famous Captain Book
(A distant cousin of Captain Hook),
In his cabin quietly read,
And as his ship rode through the waves
In pages there he hid his head.

His crew were avid readers too,
Of daring pirate tales,
Stories 'bout the briny sea,
Filled with great white whales.

And on and on their ship did sail,
Past lands and sands, exotic birds.
But still they noticed none of this—
Their books they much preferred.

Till . . . the captain paused and
    looked around.
He'd finished one more book,
And noticing his socks were wet,
He gave a quizzical look.

A cabin full of water!
His ship was full of holes.
Then realizing, "Bookworms!
We're sinking! Save your souls!"

And down and down that ship did sink,
A stone it was indeed.
Though still the crew they hardly knew,
As lots there was to read.

And though the books are soaking wet,
In fact, quite waterlogged,
Today they still read on and on,
Those literate old sea dogs,

While Captain Book blows bubbles,
And each fish now discovers,
The stories of the seven seas
Between those soggy covers.

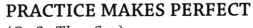

PRACTICE MAKES PERFECT
(Or So They Say)

They say with gymnastics
It's all about practice,

So I swung and swung and swung
Till my head it reeled and spun.

Down to the ground and up to the sun,
I swung and swung and swung,

And swung and swung and swung
   and swung . . .
But perhaps that was something
   I shouldn't have done?

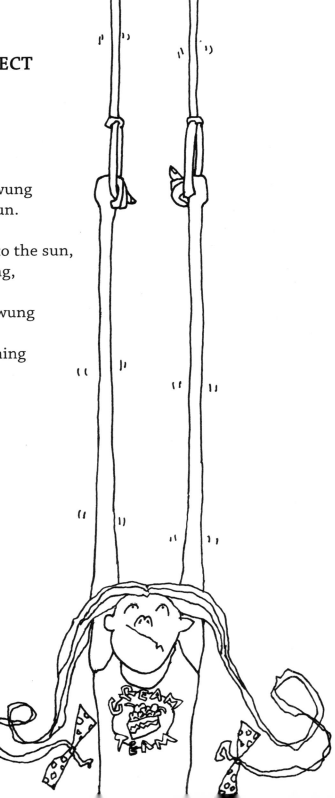

PERKY

I bet you've never seen
A sleeping coffee bean.
They're always wide awake,
They never take a break,
A little nap, a simple snooze—
Their beds they never use.
Frisky, perky through and through.
If I were made of coffee, though, I'd be perky too!

TERRIBLE NEWS
FROM THE CATERPILLAR ZOO

The Wiggle Zoo is empty.
Thieves have broken in—
A very smart, professional ring—
And stolen everything.

Some say they saw a flash
Of blossoms in the spring.
Some say they heard a flutter, flap—
The sound of tiny wings.

But flutter? Flap? What's that?
It's really quite absurd.
The strangest thing I've ever heard—
Caterpillars aren't birds!

The thieves, they're still at large,
But when they're caught I'll bet
They've sold those little cuddly things
As creepy-crawly pets.

Though something is amiss,
There's not a single clue,
'Cept blooms of spring, the sound of wings,
And one real empty zoo.

Just cages in a row,
A leaf upon the floor.
A master plan, the perfect crime,
A mystery for sure.

MR. TOMORROW

Unbelievably wise,
A genius in disguise,
A prophet of backward foresight,
A brain extremely bright.
The man who invented left-handed toothpaste,
Plums with a strawberry taste,
Fairy-tale-telling pillows,
Handkerchiefs for weeping willows,
Umbrella-hats for when it rains,
Hair curlers for lions' manes,
The everlasting bar of soap,
Self-knotting rope,
And things of such far-reaching vision
As the Which-Century-Are-We-In Watch
And the toenail television.

Oh, if only I were him,
The inventor of water wings
For fish who can not swim,
Of alarm clocks for dormant flowers
To note the seasonal hour.
Small white canes for bats,
Dog-repellant cream for cats,
Reading glasses that write as well,
And socks that never smell.

Yes, this is the man they call Mr. Tomorrow.
If only (for one minute) his brain I could borrow!

WHY ITALIANS EAT NOODLES
AND NOT POODLES

They say Marco Polo traveled East
In search of things to eat,
Having heard that in those lands
There were treats, deliciously sweet.
Like the scrumptious Chinese miniature poodle
That surely they'd love back home
On account of its scrump-ti-osity
In the cafes of Venice and Rome.
But as those miniature poodles
Were so unbelievably small,
Marco Polo couldn't find a single one at all.
So instead of poodles,
He brought back noodles!

And after he'd covered those noodles in tomato sauce
And renamed them "spaghetti,"
The whole of Italy celebrated
By dancing and throwing confetti.

And that's why today Italians eat spaghetti,
Or should I say Chinese noodles,
Instead of yapping "pedigree plates"
Of cuddly miniature poodles.
(Covered, of course, in tomato sauce!)

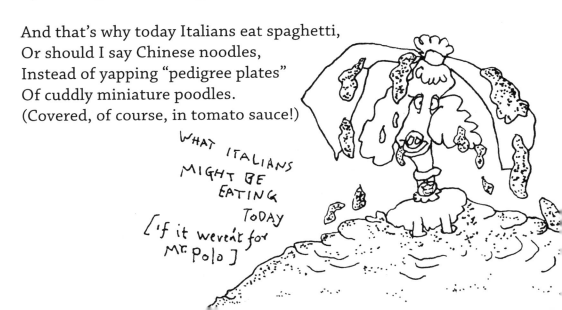

WHAT ITALIANS
MIGHT BE
EATING
TODAY
['f it weren't for
Mr. Polo]

THE FUSS ABOUT AN OCTOPUS

The Giant Arctic Octopus
Is one you must
Not ever trust,

That is, if you're some Eskimo,
Sitting by your fishing hole,
Somewhere near the ol' North pole.

For like the iceberg in the sea,
Most of it you cannot see,

Except for one small tentacle that in the air appears
And gives a little wiggle when Eskimos are near.

As if to say, "Yoo hoo! Hello!"
Then oh dear, oh . . . no Eskimo!

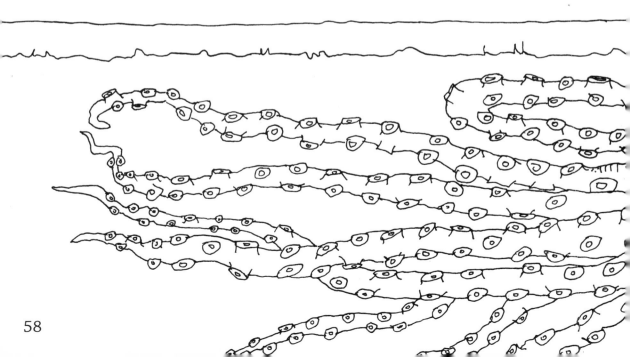

No eski-nose, no eski-toe—
Nothing but an eski-"Noooooo!"

A hole, a pole, the ice and snow,
And lunch or dinner down below.

So there . . . and now I've let you know,
You and any Eskimo,

The Giant Arctic Octopus
Is one you must
Not ever trust.

THE FARMER OF FANTASTIC FIELDS

Oh I will go and farm the sea
With tractors, trucks, and plows,
And far across those soggy lands
Sow meadows for my cows,
Who'll wear their water wings and moo,
And float and frolic through the blue.

Oh I will go and farm the sky
And in the clouds I'll grow
Cauliflower and beans and sprouts
And carrots, row by row,
While hanging heavy in the air
Orchard fruit will ripen there.

And I will farm the Milky Way—
Plant peas among the stars,
Pluto pumpkins, Venus vines,
Mega-melons on Mars—
Then rocket race them to the stores,
Freshly picked from cosmic shores.

Ah, but first I'll farm the universe
That lies inside of me,
Where one small seed, a bright idea,
Can grow a giant tree.
And there'll be treasures to behold,
Worth more than hills of solid gold.

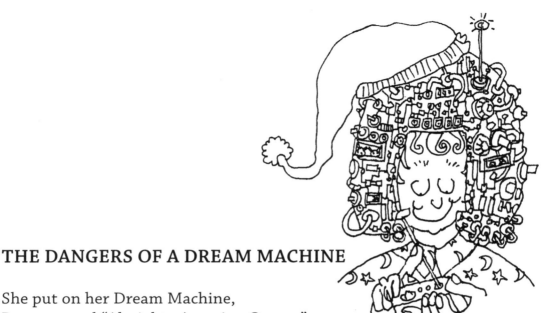

THE DANGERS OF A DREAM MACHINE

She put on her Dream Machine,
Programmed "Almighty Amazing Queen,"
Got into bed,
And pressed the button that read:
"FIGHTING ALIENS FROM PLANET ZOOZ."
But instead of pressing "WIN,"
She mistakenly pressed "LOSE."

So now she's buried to her head
(Far from the snugness of her bed)
In awful smelly alien stew
Upon that distant Planet Zooz,
Guarded by a zombie crew—
50-legged and spotted blue.

Oh dear, oh dear, oh dear, oh what is a girl to do?

P.S.
Oh, and if you happen to own such a hi-tech dream machine
And really want to be an intergalactic king or queen,
Perhaps it's best to press "SWEET" when you program a dream!

THE LIGHT OF YOUR LIFE

In fog, in mist,
On winter nights
When all is raven black,
Try this—the "Little Lighthouse Kit,"
With suction pad and battery pack.
When streets are poorly lit,
Or starless are the roads you roam,
Here's a light to guide your way
And lead you safely home.

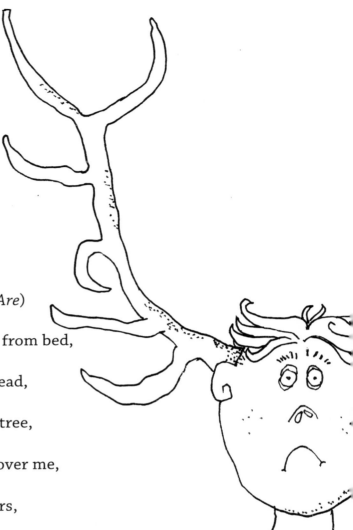

DEER ME

(What You Say Is What You Are)

This morning when I leapt from bed,
Oh deer, oh deer, oh deer,
I found I'd antlers on my head,
Oh deer, oh deer, oh deer.
Like leafless branches of a tree,
Oh deer, oh deer, oh deer,
They swayed and towered over me,
Oh deer, oh deer, oh deer,
Great aerials behind my ears,
Oh deer, oh deer, oh deer,
A crown of thorny sharpened spears,
Oh deer, oh deer, oh deer.
What next, I thought—a bright red nose,
Oh deer, oh deer, oh deer,
And little hooves where once were toes?
Oh deer, oh deer, oh deer.
But what, at last, confirmed my fear,
Oh deer, *oh deer,* ***oh deer,*** **OH DEER,**
Was when I heard a sleigh draw near!
Oh deer, oh deer, oh deer.

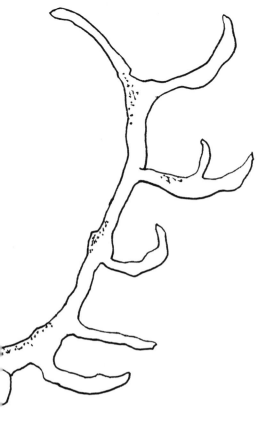

SPRING FASHION

The shoe store said, "They'll give you
That light and airy feeling."
So home she went
And tried them on
And walked straight through the ceiling!

THE GREAT AFRICAN DINNER DANCE

As dusk comes to the water hole,
Before the land grows dark as coal,

Dance the lions, young and old,
The mighty kings, so brave and bold,

Putting on their Evening Show
Of knotted tail and padded toe

To entertain the sleek gazelle,
Made moon-eyed by a magic spell,

And in the theater—*The Golden Mane*—
Act One begins, "The Safari Plain."

The Waltz of Wild and Whiskered Races,
The Savannah Samba of Open Spaces,
The Four-Paw Polka, The Ostrich Nest,
The Endless Horizon East to West.

While Joe Flamingo on one stick
Gazes at the slow-quick-quick,

And those in polished high-heeled hooves
Are mesmerized by clever moves,

A treat each family can enjoy—
Gnu, giraffe, and zebra boy.

The Hippo Hop, The Bush-Land Twirl,
The Dance of Dust, The Untamed Whirl,
The Jungle Jig, The Squawking Bird,
The Rumba of the Running Herd.

As warthogs with their muddy feet,
The great bewildered wildebeest,

Grunt and squeal and loudly bellow
At this blur of brilliant yellow.

A kick of legs, a glimpse of red,
The toss of each majestic head,

And thus in this, the Sunset Hour,
They pad and pose their repertoire.

The Dance of White and Shining Teeth,
The Merry Mask (What Lies Beneath),
The Great and Growling Tummy Feast,
The Quick-Step of the Starving Beast.

Till down there by the water hole,
Across the sky the bright stars stroll,

And there our audience on that shore
Screams and shrieks, "ENCORE! ENCORE!"

For Dance of Claws and Open Jaws,
The Slow and Loving Lick of Paws.

But can it be the guests get bored
By these our players, the Dancing Lords?

For still when comes the curtain call,
The grand finale, *The Mighty Roar,*

Strange but you can be quite sure
Our audience is no more!

ALMIGHTY JOKER

Why's the banana skin so slippery?
Is it Our Maker's idea of playfulness or trickery?
For when I've gone and slipped on one,
I've heard a lot of "**HA, HA, HA's**"
From far, far, far past Venus, Mars—
Way past the distant stars.

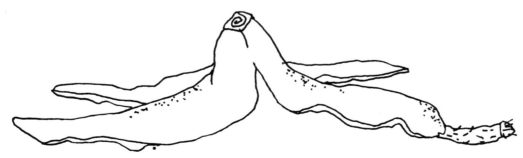

(Dropped by one of the Pigyou Tribe.)

SEEDY CHARACTER

To get that "natural look,"
He took some seeds and shook
A handful on his hairless head,
And then he went to bed.

And waking at the crack of dawn,
He found that he had grown a lawn,
And all he needed now to know
Was when to water, when to mow.

THE LAST OF THE
GREAT COSMIC TEA SET

It's only flying saucers that
We ever seem to see
And never matching cups or plates—
That's very strange to me.

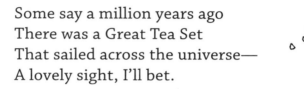

Some say a million years ago
There was a Great Tea Set
That sailed across the universe—
A lovely sight, I'll bet.

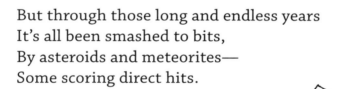

But through those long and endless years
It's all been smashed to bits,
By asteroids and meteorites—
Some scoring direct hits.

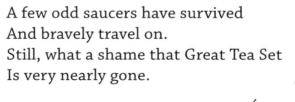

A few odd saucers have survived
And bravely travel on.
Still, what a shame that Great Tea Set
Is very nearly gone.

71

JOGGING WITH JUNIOR

What a big to-do,
If, like kangaroos,
Our moms had little pouches—
Oh what a lot of ouches!

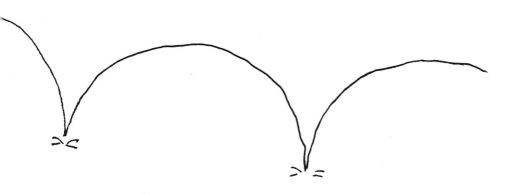

SUPER SNOUT, THE FORTUNE SMELLER

No strange mysterious cards,
No crystal ball,
No charts of the starry heavens—
Nothing like that at all.
For Madame Super Snout, the Fortune Smeller,
Can smell the future, everyone 'll tell ya,
As if it were a scented rose,
Simply by using her giant nose.

Just one sniff,
And she can tell you if
You'll be a banker, baker, or candlestick maker.
She can smell tomorrow, and next week,
   a hundred years ahead.
She can smell what grades you'll get in school,
     and who you're going to wed . . .
Smell the name of your husband, your future wife.
She can smell every detail about your life.

But . . . well, the particular day I went
To Madame Super Snout's darkened tent,
I think she must have had a terrible cold,
'Cause this is what I was told:

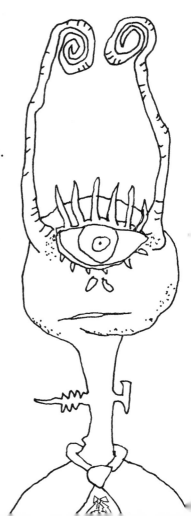

"Ah, my dear,
I don't see you fitting in down here,
Down here on planet Earth.
I see you somewhere else in the great big universe,
Happily married to a blob of green,
(The most beautiful blob you've ever seen).
With lots of little ones, blob after blob,
And you're settled down at a well-paid job,
The one you've often dreamed of too,
Far off on some celestial moon
Filling shoes with sticky goo
From morning until afternoon."

Filling shoes with sticky goo?
Huh! That's definitely not what I'm going to do!
Umm, I don't know what ol' Super Snout smelled
(Maybe my socks—the ones from hell!),
But there's one thing I can tell you now,
And don't ask me why I know, or how,
Either she's an utter long-nosed fake,
Or she made a horrible mistake.
Just look at me. I'm not someone you can deceive.
I mean, is that something you'd believe?
Really, a wife that's just a blob of green?
(Though the most beautiful blob I've even seen),
That's a future I really don't need.
What nonsense, indeed!

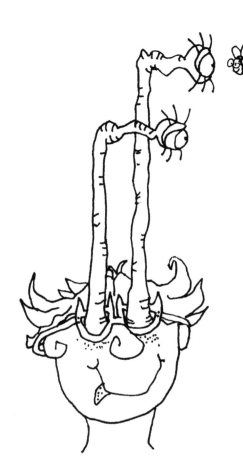

LONG LOOK

Of course, there are the eyes of owls
Or those of hovering hawks,
But I'd like to have the eyes of a snail
On the end of long, long stalks

For peering over fence or hedge,
Perhaps the neighbor's wall.
And then I wouldn't have to stand
On tippy-toes at all

When trying to see the queen go by
In her shiny limousine,
Or cheering at a crowded game
My favorite football team.

Okay, okay, it's just as I feared,
You're right . . . I'd look pretty weird!

THE FANTASTIC CURLY-WHIRLY
FUTURISTIC FRENCH HORN

Be warned—
Patience is a virtue
When playing this horn.
So take a deep breath,
Fill your cheeks,
Bloooooooow, and then
Wait several weeks . . .
Or perhaps a month, a couple of years,
For a single note to reach your ears.

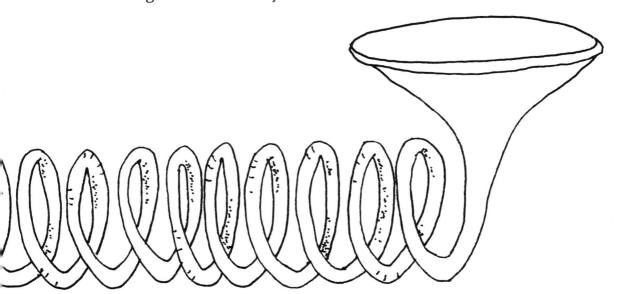

TONGUE-TIED

It's awful when chameleon friends
Their mouths snap open wide,
And chasing after one small fly . . .
Their sticky tongues collide!

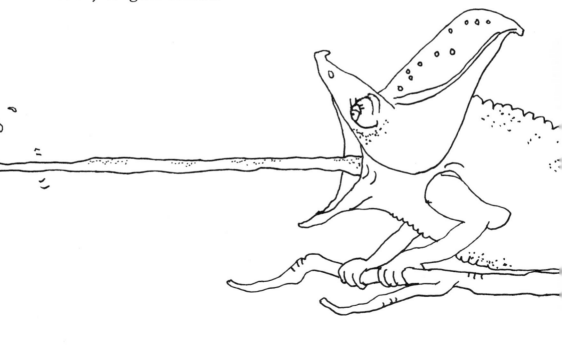

HOW TO TELL A CROCODILE
FROM AN ALLIGATOR BY
THE WAY IT SAYS GOODBYE

The crocodile cries and dries its eyes
With lots of sobs and sniffs and sighs,

While the oh so friendly alligator
Winks and waves, "I'll see you later."

Crocodiles cry, alligators lie,
But either way . . . bye-bye!

(And who cares if they cried or lied
When you're down there inside.)

EASY ANGLING

"Today I'm fishing for compliments
With this unusual bait.

Yes, all I need to use
Is a very heavy weight."

"Gosh, to go and fish with that
You must be *really* strong!"

"See, to catch a compliment
I never wait that long!"

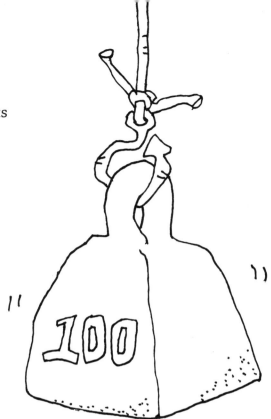

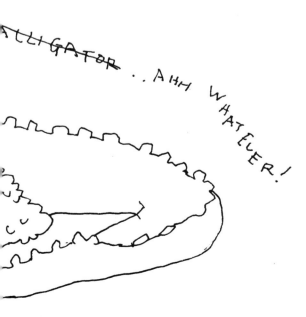

ALLIGATOR .. AHH WHATEVER!

PEA TIME

I've trained a fresh bread roll to roll,
A rambling rose to stay at home,
A pair of specs to ride a nose,
And toes to dance in rows.

Now I'm training a garden pea,
Not to . . . well, it's clear to see.
For as you've guessed, it's not learned yet—
It still keeps getting the carpet wet!

THE PERFECT PET

The pretty patterned carpet's
The perfect pet for sure.
It lies upon the floor
Or flat out by the door.
You never have to feed it
Or walk it in the park.
All you do is leave it,
It never bites or barks.

Surprisingly, though, the carpet
Doesn't like cars one bit,
'Cause maybe in a car
It's really hard to fit.
(Rolled up, that is, inside of it.)
It much prefers your room,
Just staring at the ceiling.
And even if you tread on it,
You'll never hurt its feelings.

But if by chance it's naughty,
Then here's the thing to do—
Simply take it from the room
And beat it with a broom.

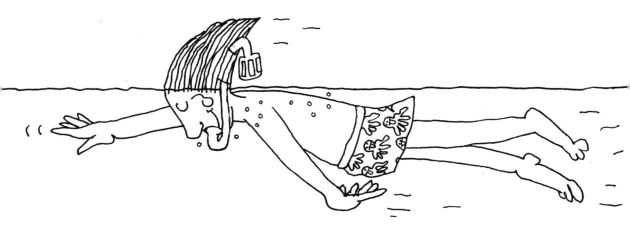

ALONE AT LAST

Want to swim in peace?
Want all that seaside noise to cease?
Want to float in crystal blue?
Without the crowds, and surfboards too?
Then here's the very thing for you—
The Scary Shark Hairdo!

BUBBLING BIRD

Now to tell
Of this winged shell,
The tiny turtle dove
That never ever flies above
The clouds, but further down.
In fact, far further down
In Davy Jones's Town.
And there among the salty skies,
The seaweed trees, the oyster beds,
It slowly puffs and paddles on
And nods its feathered head,
And sings its song, a song gone wrong—
A cooing bubbling sound.
The strangest bird for miles around,
This bird that never drowns.

THE BIG CHEESE
(*And the Mice with the Trembling Knees*)

The Big Cheese towered—an office block,
A huge and smelly yellow rock,
A mighty fuming cheesy chunk,
The "perfume" of a year-old sock.

And all the naughty little mice
Looked up at that great fearful cheese,
A cheese that made their blood quite freeze,
That made them tremble, tail to knees.

For Big Cheese raged and gnashed and roared,
"Yes, I'm the king of Cheesendom.
The golden cheese that blocks the sun.
The cheese that weighs a thousand tons."

Yes, here was quite a wedge of cheese—
An evil, ugly, awful sight.
A great big bully, gangster type,
A monster both of weight and height.

And there it roared, "I've come to fight,
To seek revenge for all my friends,
Who lived and loved and smiled and smelled
But sadly came to cheesy ends.

By you, you nibblers of the night,
You furry bags on little feet.
But now it's time to feel my teeth,
For now your Maker you shall meet!"

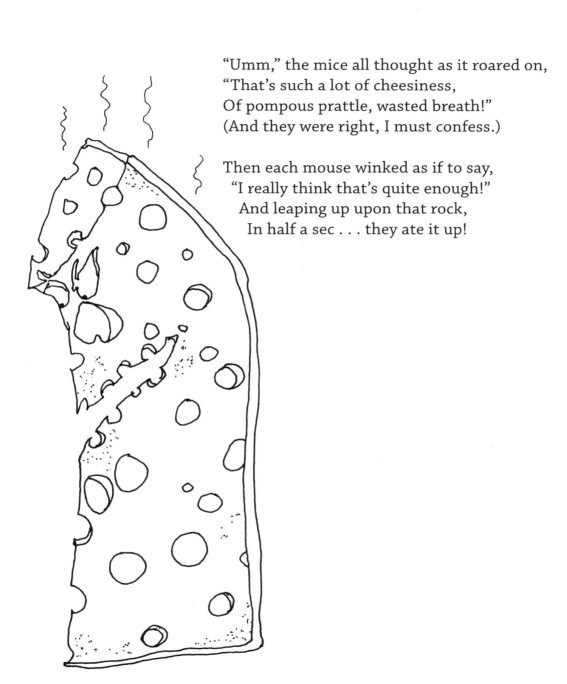

"Umm," the mice all thought as it roared on,
"That's such a lot of cheesiness,
Of pompous prattle, wasted breath!"
(And they were right, I must confess.)

Then each mouse winked as if to say,
  "I really think that's quite enough!"
  And leaping up upon that rock,
    In half a sec . . . they ate it up!

EAR ART

Salvador Balmi's most famous painting
Is surely "The Walls Have Ears"—
A masterpiece of experimentation,
The envy of his peers.

P.S.
Other paintings in the same series include
"The Bedroom Ceiling Has Toes"
and "My Nose Without Its Clothes."

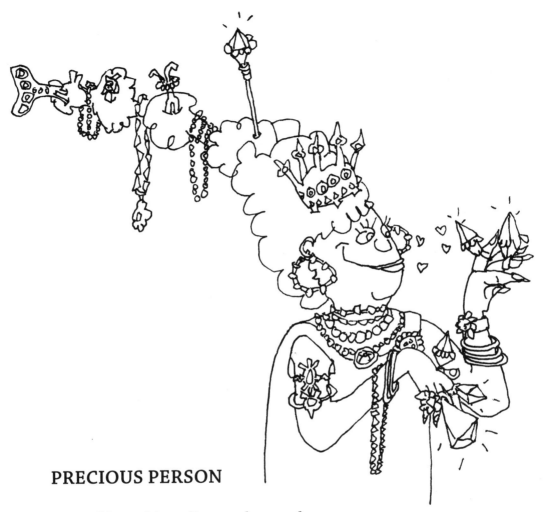

PRECIOUS PERSON

Emeralds, rubies, diamonds, pearls,
Sapphires by the score.
On every finger, precious gems—
A treasure chest she wore.

Though someone should have warned her,
Stopped her, gently told her
About the dangers 'round the corner . . .
Too late—someone stole her!

THE SOUND OF SWEETNESS

The Bango Mango is said to be sweet,
A juicy scrumptious delectable treat.
But actually no one really knows,
For when you bite it—it explodes!

GNOME SWEET GNOME

In the garden of a home,
There stands a happy smiling gnome
Who never grumbles or complains,
Even when it snows or rains,
But stands there smiling all alone.
And if perhaps the truth be known,
We'd find some wisdom of our own
If sometimes *we* were made of stone.

SHELL-SHOCKED
The Tale of Twenty Thousand Snails
(*Or How the Pied Piper Became the Tired Piper*)

Slitherville, so goes the tale,
Was plagued by twenty thousand snails.
Snails that slithered down the street,
Crawled up walls, and over feet.
Across the floor, beneath the bed,
In shoes, up legs, atop your head.

But what to do? Oh what to do?
The townsfolk didn't have a clue,
Till they recalled that Piper's whistle
And how all creatures seemed to listen
To that man (more batty than bats)—
The one who rid that town of rats.
And so they called him up to ask,
"Hey, how about another task?"
And taking out his little flute
He blew a magic "toot, toot, toot"
That made those snails both far and near
Prick up each tiny snaily ear
And slither slowly (rain or shine)
In one great slimy monster line
Behind the Piper as he played
His "Tooting Song" throughout the day.

But when it comes to snails and slime,
You really can forget the time,
And he that once was known as Pied
Is now the Tired, the bleary-eyed.
For though he blows that trusty whistle,
And those snails, I'm sure, still listen,
Now his tune is faint and weak
After several hundred weeks—
'Cause still those friends around his feet
Are only . . . HALFWAY DOWN THE STREET!

(And when, of course, I think of that,
Perhaps he should have stuck to rats!)

THE BEAUTY OF THE BEAST

They say that leopards never change their spots,
But if they did, perhaps to squiggles and dots,
Blotches and splodges of strawberry cream,
Swirls of purple and olive green,
Then in a tree, you'd have to agree,
They'd be very easily seen.

ONE QUIRKY TURKEY

The most argumentative bird in all the world
Is the Two-Headed Chatterbox Turkey,
One that indeed can be called quite quirky.
For when it goes and gobbles,
With itself it continually squabbles,
And though two heads are said to be much better than one,
In the case of the Chatterbox Turkey,
   that's absolutely wrong.

WHAT LITTLE SQUIRTS
COULD DO TO BIG BULLIES

If only we did
The same as the ocean squid,
Who, when in a tight spot, squirts out ink—
That would stop bullying in school, I think!

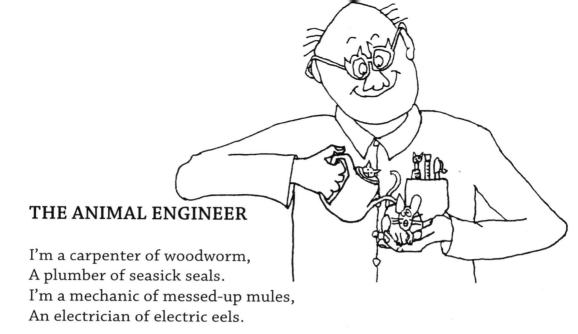

THE ANIMAL ENGINEER

I'm a carpenter of woodworm,
A plumber of seasick seals.
I'm a mechanic of messed-up mules,
An electrician of electric eels.

In fact, if you have an animal or pet that's broken down,
Or that makes a weird purring or gulping sound,
Just call me, I'm the fastest fixer around.

I can tune old raspy crows,
Straighten an anteater's nose,
Service a smelly skunk,
Unblock an elephant's trunk,
Mend dogs with lopsided licks,
Fix a flea that ticks,
An ostrich whose head is stuck in the sand,
A snake that cannot stand.

At the moment I'm fixing a mouse that squeaks,
But you say you have a shark that leaks?
Well, I'm booked up for several weeks,
But if you think that it might sink . . .
Well, let me see, in an emergency
I suppose I could visit your house . . .

But first, let me oil this mouse.

BIG DECISION
ON THE ROAD OF LIFE

Coming to a fork in the road
He wondered which way to go.
Umm . . . eeny, meeny, miney, mo,
Or should the wind just blow?

By brightest day and darkest night
He'd traveled long and far,
And on the way he'd learned in life,
Many decisions there are.

But here was surely the greatest yet.
He stood and scratched his head.
Er . . . should he perhaps go to the left
Or should he go right instead?

POP POETRY

"BOOM! BOOM! BOOM!" went Balloon Boy's heart
On seeing Cactus Kate.
But no one told him love would hurt
Or worse, much worse (just wait!)
Perhaps it was the hand of fate,
But anyway . . . too late!

ROCK FOX

(The Hard—Very Hard—Luck Story
of the Fox and the Cement Mixer)

One day a fox, Miss Trixie,
Fell in love with "Mister Mixy"
(Handsome, strong, from heaven sent,
Filled with sloppy fresh cement).

"Oh please, oh please, just one quick kiss,"
Insisted pretty Foxy Miss,
But Mister Mixy turned his head
And looked the other way instead.

"Oh please, oh please, just one quick kiss,"
Our Foxy Miss repeated this.
So Mixy turned and promptly . . . kissed her!
(He really was a romantic mixer.)

But then he turned (and churned) away.
"Happy now?" he seemed to say,
While though Miss Trixie loved that mixer . . .

Nothing much could fix her!

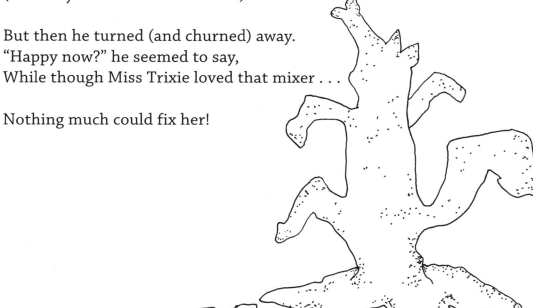

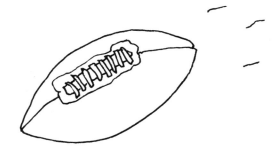

THE FLY-BY FLOWER

The sunflower
    Stretches
        For the sun,
            To grasp
                That ball
                    Of brilliant light.
                    But this flower
                        Stretches
                            Left
                                And right,
                                    To follow
                                        Whatever
                                            It finds
                                                In flight.

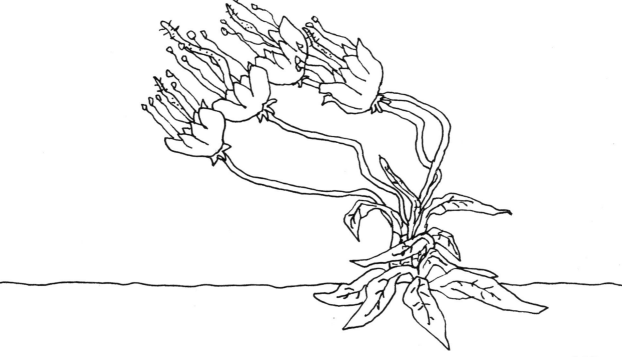

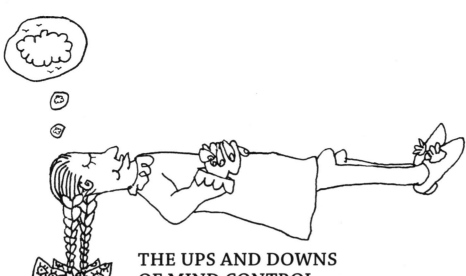

THE UPS AND DOWNS
OF MIND CONTROL

I'm learning how to levitate,
To float into the air,
Imagining myself a cloud.
Oh, watch the people stare

As up and up and up I go,
Skyward bound above the town.
Still, this part I can do with ease,
The problem's coming down.

For now I have to think of things
Like anvils, rocks, the kitchen sink.
But of that lightning journey down,
I try hard n
      o
       o
       o
       o
       o
       t
         to think!

DIZZY DRINKING

Whenever I drink a cup of tea,
A galaxy of stars I see.
I feel I'm spinning—spiraling through
The universe—I'm dizzy too.
But why should tea
Do this to me?
I haven't got a clue!

Have you?

(Designed by the same person
who designed the Futuristic French Horn.)

THE DUNCE OF THE HIVE

The little Spelling Bee
Loves to buzz along,
Spelling words upon the air . . .

(Though every one's spelled wrong!)

A MESSAGE FROM
HUMPTY DUMPTY'S MOTHER

When
I met the hen
That laid Humpty Dumpty on that wall
(Not the best place to lay an egg for sure),
And told her that he'd had a fall,
And that all the king's horses and all the king's men
Couldn't put Humpty together again,
She clucked, "It's no fun being a hen
When even the horses and all the king's men
Can't put your eggs back together again.
In fact I've just laid another one, friend,
On the road around the bend.
But if my eggs they still can't mend,
I'm never going to lay one . . . ever again!"

MRS. DUMPTY

SCHOOL OF PHEW

Consider Kung Phew, that martial art,
Whose students from the very start
Are not allowed to bathe or shower.
(It's said to clean off all their power!)
Who never change their clothes for years
Or ever wash behind their ears,
Who have a mighty knockout strength,
A suffocating self-defense.
In fact, it's said by pose alone
They make opponents moan and groan,
And "stinky stuff" instead of kicks
Can break a pile of bricks.

IN THE LAND OF MODERN MANNERS

When women laughed in ancient Japan,
In front of their mouths they placed their hands
Or perhaps an open fan.

But now the Japanese,
An inventive people for certain,
Have exchanged those hands and fans . . .
For a charming little curtain!

THE EMPEROR'S OLD CLOTHES
(*A Poem for Those with High IQs*)

Of course you know the story
Of the emperor's brand-new clothes—
The ones he proudly wore
As through the streets he rode,
The ones that only the clever could see
(And that means you and me!),
Until some little smarty pants went and shouted out,
"Hey, look, the king's not wearing a single thing!"
And the emperor (or was he really king?)
Realizing his subjects had heads like knotted string
And couldn't see his pants, his coat,
(And weren't so smart, as you will note),
Removed himself from all the fuss,
And went straight home in quiet disgust.

But that's only half the story, you know.

I was passing the palace just the other day,
When hey, lo and behold,
There in the bin were those same ol' clothes,
Covered in dirt and regal mold
So . . . not to look a gift horse in the mouth,
Of course, I took them out,
Dusted them down.
(I even found a crown!)
And look, tra-la—here they are!
As good as new.
And . . . if you wait a second or two
I'll try them on for you!

Hey, whoa! Whoa! Where y' going? Where y' going?
Okay, so they need some sewing,
But . . . er . . .

(Umm . . . you're not as smart as I thought you were!)

'COURSE YOU CAN SEE THE CLOTHES . . . RIGHT?

THE GREAT COVER-UP
(*An Ode to Extra-Quick-Growing Ivy*)

Ivy, ivy,
Very lively.
Harmless little shoot.

Green and cute,
Leaf to root . . .

What an awful brute!

5 minutes later

THE ODD ONE IN THE ORCHARD
(A Poem I Especially Picked for You)

Oh Jenny Jamjar, yes you are
The apple of my eye,
The mango of each ripened ear—
I cannot tell a lie.
The juicy peach of my big toe
The grapefruit of my knee.
Oh what a most peculiar tree
You've gone and made of me!

SLOW, SLOW, QUICK,
QUICK QUICKSAND

Hey, slow down, quicksand, be my guest—
Use my sofa, have a rest.

Hey, slow down, quicksand, hit the brakes—
Slam them on for heaven's sake.

Hey, slow down, quicksand, check your speed—
"Halt" it says, or can't you read?

Hey, slow down, quicksand, hold it, wait—
No one cares if sand is late.

Hey, slow down, quicksand, I beseech—
Can't you be a nice ol' beach?

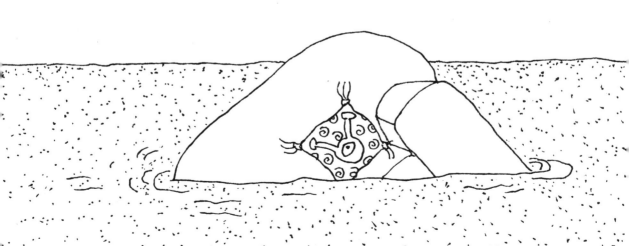

Hey, slow down, quicksand, aren't you hot?
Turbo-cheetah, that you're not.

Hey, slow down, quicksand, don't you care
How the tortoise beat the hare?

Hey, slow down, quicksand, stay 'n' play—
Sniff the roses 'long the way.

Hey, slow down, quicksand, I don't mind—
Lie about, relax, unwind.

Hey, slow down, quicksand, stay for tea—
But please make sure that tea's not me!

PARROT POST

I'm starting a special service—parrot post,
Messages delivered from coast to coast.
But unlike pigeons
With messages tied to their feet,
My parrots are unique—
They fly to you . . . and speak!
(First class, two days; Second, a week.)

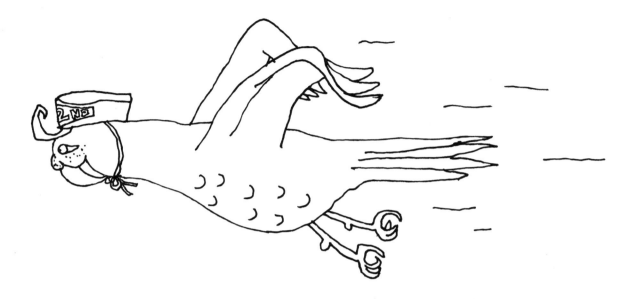

MOTHER FOUR-EYES

My mom says she has eyes in the back of her head
And can see whatever I do,

And by the look of her special specs
I think what she says is true,

Don't you?

KIDNAPPED CAT

In the National Museum of Mars
There's a cat in a small glass case.
Underneath is written:
"A SAMPLE OF THE HUMAN RACE."
Isn't it amazing how a simple mistake
Becomes the truth in another place?
(And that's not just in outer space!)

"A SAMPLE OF THE
HUMAN RACE"
(in Martian!) →

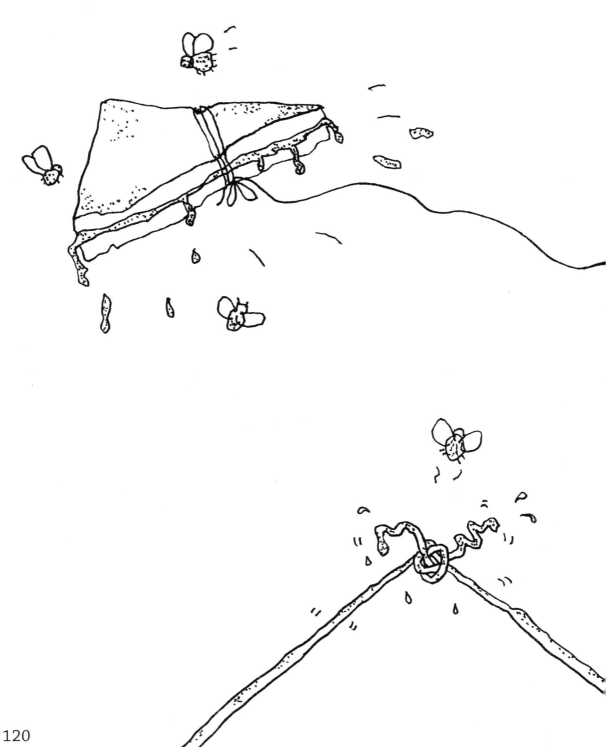

THE ART OF FLY FISHING

Of course you know fly fishing
Is fishing for a fly
By hurling a jam sandwich
High into the sky.
A very skillful art
To catch that buzzing fly
(In fact, not one but ninety-nine),
And then head home and proudly dine
On freshly baked fly pie!

AN UNBUTTONED LIFE
IS NOT NICE
(*Nor Is It a Pleasant Sight*)

If one minute you're running around and having fun,
And the next you're unraveling and becoming completely undone,
Splitting apart at the seams, and it seems
   there's something terribly wrong,
And looking down you realize "Uh-oh, my bellybutton's gone!"
(The most important button ever—
   the one that keeps you all together.)
Well, you'd better run and tell your mom
And get her to give you another one.
And ask her to quickly sew it on
Before (and this I know for sure)
Everything starts dropping to the floor,
And all that you own
Falls off your bones
And ends in a pile of assorted parts
Like a very nice piece of modern art.

And now you know,
This only goes to show
That without that button (unlike a tooth)
All comes loose—and that's the truth.

So if, by chance, yours does come off,
Well, here's a piece of nice advice—
Sew on that new one *really* tight.
It might . . .

Just save your life!

IF ONLY

I sat counting pebbles on the shore,
Till I reached two thousand and sixty-four
   and then became bored.
So I counted the waves on the great wide sea
Till I reached three thousand and thirty-three
   and that became tedious to me.
So I began to count leaves on every tree,
But when I'd reached almost infinity
   I was suddenly called for tea.

Oh if only I hadn't got bored,
If only my mother hadn't called,
If only I'd kept on counting those pebbles,
   those waves, those leaves,
Till I'd counted one and all.
Just think how wise I'd be—
The Master of Life's Great Mysteries.

Oh dearie, dearie me—
If only I hadn't been called for tea.

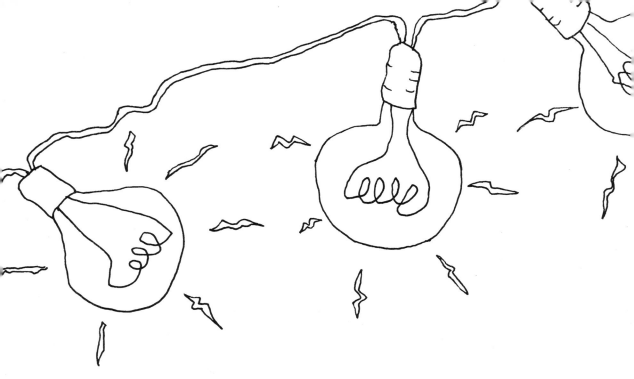

COSMIC ENERGY CRISIS

I've heard it said that stars
Are ships in cosmic seas,
With all their starboard lanterns lit
To sail that astral breeze.

But I say they're huge light bulbs
Up there burning bright,
Left on and forgotten in
The Bedroom of the Night.

And look, they're burning still!
And maybe always will
Till someone up there, one fine day,
Gets the electric bill!

THE REASON WHY ALIENS
ALWAYS SEEM TO BE GREEN

With a whizzzzzzz,   a whooooosh,   a wheeeeee

Across vast galaxies
They sail those choppy cosmic skies
Crawling on their knees,

Or heads poked out the windows
Of supersonic ships.
Oh, how their tummies rumble on
Those long galactic trips!

At triple light-year speeds
They cruise that starry sea,
All bug-eyed, groggy, vivid green—
As sick as sick can be.

THE FLY WHO DEFIED THE SAMURAI

The samurai—the Master of the Sword.
The samurai—loyal to shogun, lord.
The samurai—whom no one can defy,
Unless, of course, they want to . . . die!

But there there sat a little fly,
Upon that mighty samurai.
Between the swordsman's steely eyes—
A fly that had to die!

A fly that seemed to have no fears
(Perhaps because it had no ears)
And could not hear that swordsman's cry:
"You dare defy the samurai?
Take flight or you will die!"

But still the fly it did defy
That brave and mighty samurai
And sat there quite oblivious
To all the noise and fuss.

"Ah so, you fly, you still defy
The mighty samurai?
A senseless, foolish duel you choose—
Your life you now shall lose!"

And with that blade of sharpened steel,
In ceremonious style he kneeled,
And with his battle cry, "**BANZAI!**"
His sword flashed down toward the fly!

Oh, my.

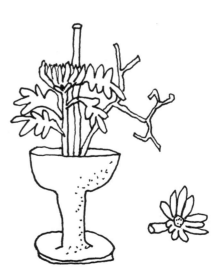

WATER WHEELS

Here it is—"The Soggy Cycle,"
My latest brilliant invention,
The underwater bicycle
With special snorkel extension!

But though I can take credit,
It's not perfected yet—
I still can't seem to ride it
Without getting soaking wet!

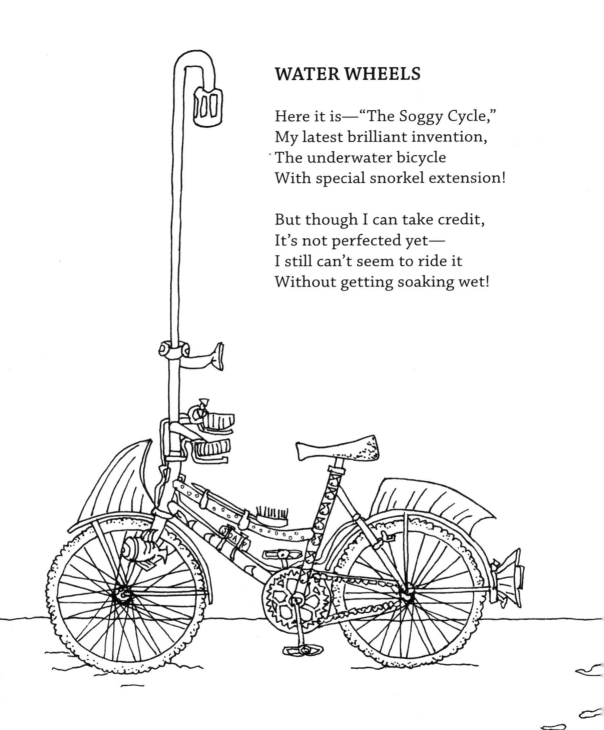

NOT AN ACORN AFTER ALL

Chicken Little never did tell the king
That the sky was about to fall.
(The king who cared for one and all—
Who'd never let the poor sky fall.)

So surprisingly, when the king awoke,
He found his crown, his shoes, his velvet cloak
All soaked in slimy, bright sky blue—
And very sticky too.

And oh, the king he had a fit!
Now Foxy Loxy's in for it.

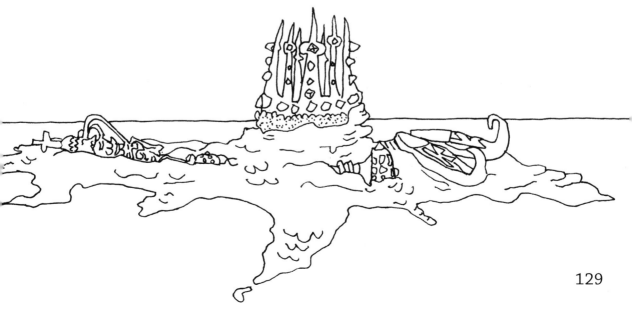

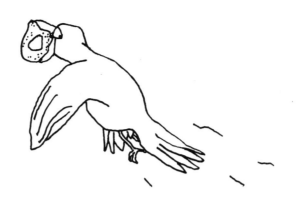

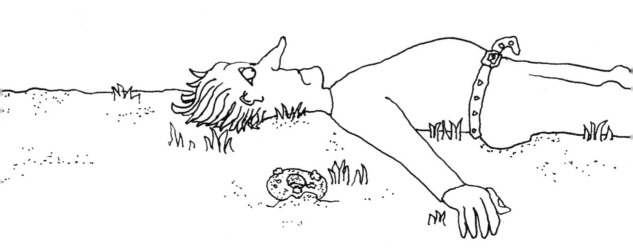

DONUTTY

Donut pitching's the latest game,
Like horseshoe pitching—the idea's the same.
A game that's played by two or more.
The winner has the highest score.
And each contestant gets three throws—
Ten points a nose and five the toes.
And one more rule, no grabbing and eating—
That's cheating!

THE LAUGHING SANDS
OF THE SA-HA-HA-HARA

Perhaps it's the wind 'cross the vast hot sands
   that makes these little chuckles.
Maybe it's the fronds of the tall palm trees
   that wave in the air and rustle.
But whatever the cause
On these desert shores,
This mysterious sound of laughter
Spells instant disaster.

Travelers fall from their camels
   and collapse in giggling fits.
Bedouin chiefs just hold their sides
   and behave like childish twits.
Arab sheiks, belly dancers, traditional desert folk
Simply can't control themselves,
   for everything's a joke.

And there they stay transfixed like that—
    beaming Cheshire cats,
Smiling inanely ear to ear,
Until . . . until . . . oh dear,
All that's left of laughter, the barrel-load of fun,
Is a great big pile of whitened bones
Under the burning sun.

BREAD HEAD

He lay and baked there in the sun,
As golden as an oven bun,

Though now and then becoming cross
When 'neath a cloud the sun was lost.

A hot cross Dough Boy on the beach
Is rather like a ripened peach,

A sweet delicious thing to eat,
In this case quite a baker's treat.

Oh Dough Boy, Dough Boy, silly you—
What a half-baked thing to do!

Now there's no one in the sun . . .
Just crumbs (no Dough Boy having fun).

And somewhere someone rubs his tum
Repeating, "Yummy! Yum, yum, yum."

CLEAN BLUE SKY

Truly modern witches
Don't use the flying broom,
But much prefer a vacuum cleaner,
And through the heavens they zooooooooooooooom.

DOOMED PLUMES

The Great Crested Eagle,
The Triple Tufted Seagull,
The Mohican Mandarin Duck,

By a stroke of real bad luck
Had to change their names—
Not to Sally, Billy, and James,

But to the Big Bald Eagle,
The Crownless Crying Seagull,
The plain ol' Plucked Mandarin Duck

When many years ago,
Or so the story goes,

Feathers (not only hens')
Were suddenly used for pens.

TELEPHONIC TREND

Miss Betsy Bopper,
The unstoppable shopper
Of every fabulous fashionable thing,
Becomes the envy
Of her friends
When her new earrings
Start to ring.

THE HEIGHT OF BEING POLITE

The sailor might talk to the sea,
But the sea, it will never talk back.
The gypsy might talk to the wind,
But the wind, it will never talk back.
The witch, she might talk to the moon,
But the moon, it will never talk back.
The moon, and the wind,
   and the waves of the sea,
Good manners they obviously lack,
For when I politely talk to myself,
At least I always talk back!

WHY JACK CAME BACK

Up 'n' up that beanstalk,
Up 'n' up Jack climbed.
Up 'n' up 'n' up
With visions in his mind—
A wondrous magic land
Where silver rivers ran,
A maiden played
A golden harp,
And to his heart
She sang.
So up
And up
Jack climbed,
Led on by all he'd find.
Up 'n' up
Into the sky,
Waving home goodbye.
But what of silver rivers?
The stuff of magic dreams?
What of girls
With golden harps?
Just melted like ice cream?
For climbing
Up 'n' onwards
In search of
Wondrous scenes,
All he ever found
Were lots
And lots of . . . beans!

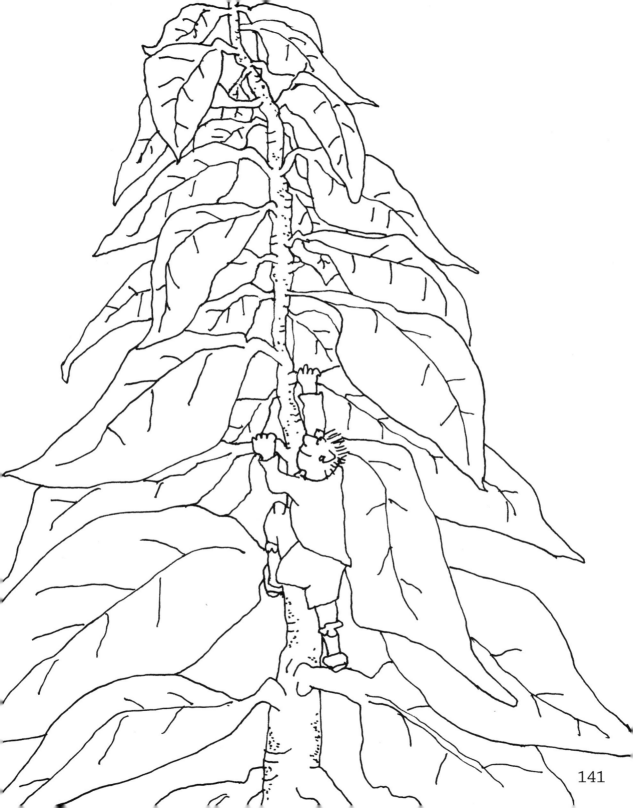

STUCK STICK

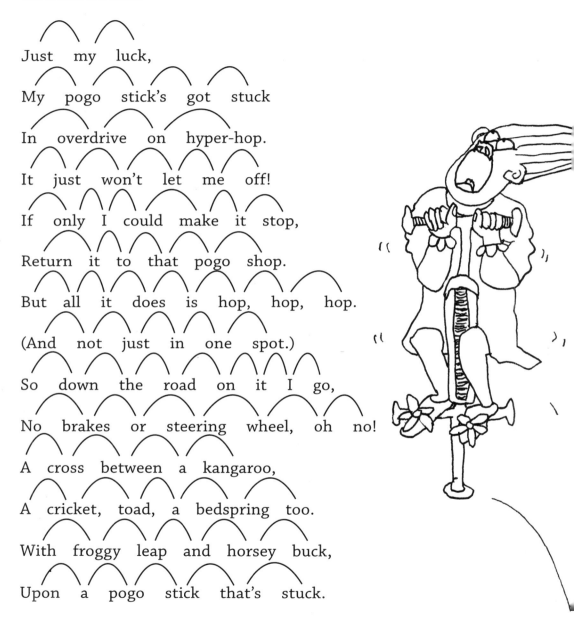

Just my luck,

My pogo stick's got stuck

In overdrive on hyper-hop.

It just won't let me off!

If only I could make it stop,

Return it to that pogo shop.

But all it does is hop, hop, hop.

(And not just in one spot.)

So down the road on it I go,

No brakes or steering wheel, oh no!

A cross between a kangaroo,

A cricket, toad, a bedspring too.

With froggy leap and horsey buck,

Upon a pogo stick that's stuck.

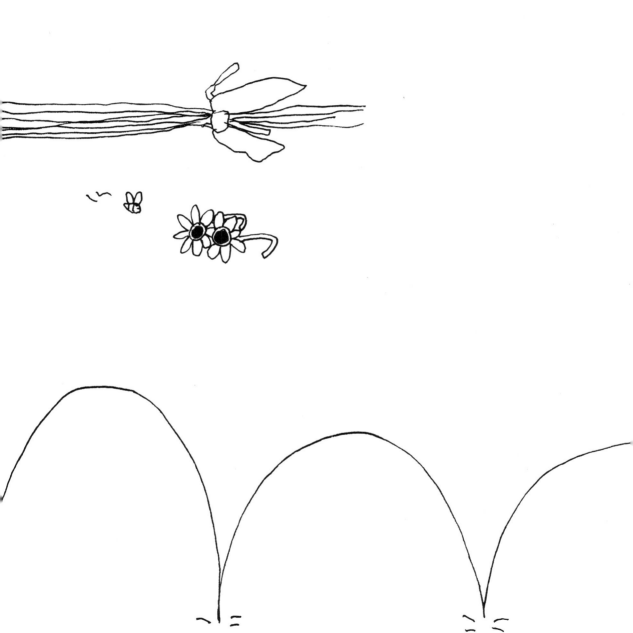

TV DINNER

The couch potato snuggled there,
So smug and satisfied,
And watched its favorite TV show
With bright eyes open wide.

When, uh-oh, to its great surprise,
A voice was heard to cry:
"Hey, what's a potato doing here?
Oh my, oh my, oh my!"

And in the time it took to blink
Those bright and twinkling eyes,
Our tater pal was (my, oh my!)
A pile of greasy fries!

(Oh, by the way,
  Aunt Enna's gone home.)

LITTLE INNOCENT ALPHABETTY

Little Innocent Alphabetty
A-B-C-D-E-F-G . . .
Loved to recite her alphabet,
H-I-J-K-L-M-N-O-P . . .
Till naturally, eventually,
She tired of X-Y-Z
And chose to recite her numbers instead
From morning till going to bed.
But better by far was the alphabet,
For now she's a bit upset.
Yes, it seems that numbers have no end—
There's always one more round the bend.
They seem to carry on and on.
(One million, nine hundred and ninety one . . .)
Oh I think our Alphabetty blundered
When she chose to recite her numbers—
(One million, nine hundred and ninety two . . .)
Umm . . . don't you?

SCRATCH ACT

The Fabulous Performing Fleas
Are an amazing act to see.
Watch them leap through flaming hoops,
Swing from a trapeze.

They're followed by that famous act,
The Doggie Duo—Rex and Patch—
Who juggle little rubber bones:
Catch . . . then scratch . . . and catch . . .
   then scratch . . .

TALL TONGUE TALE

When Ever-So-Silent-Simon was young
The cat got his tongue,
And after that
He didn't like the cat.

As a matter of fact,
He wasn't so keen on the vampire bat
(The one with the 50-foot wings),
Or the kiddy-eating eagle
(The one that gobbles things),
Or the mega-meowing tiger
(The one with the ghastly grin),
Or the terrible 10-ton shark
(The one with the sailboat fin).

And though it's rather grim,

They got the rest of him!

THE OBVIOUS

They call him Willy Forty Winks,
An obvious name, or so you'd think,
For someone always taking naps.
But as for Willy, well, perhaps
There's one more reason (hard to miss)
Just why he has a name like this.

THE BAKE-DAY SNAKE

The Apple Piethon
(Note the spelling)
Appears in kitchens smelling
Of scrumptious homemade cooking.
A snake that's always looking
For fresh-baked apple pie,
Which often tends to lie
Upon a table's edge
Or open window ledge,
Ready for a hungry snake
To slither up and take,
And in a single "GUL-UP"
Eat that pie right up.

Of course, this snake
(Which likes to eat its apples baked)
You really can't mistake.
With beady, small, puff-pastry eyes,
Surrounded by a swarm of flies,
And marked with lots of rosy dots,
And even if it's not

Well . . .

It's easy enough to spot!

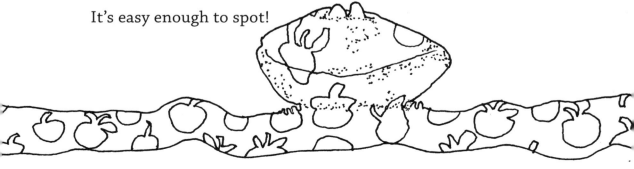

WOODWORK

The Retriever Beaver is aptly named
But hard to train when tamed.
For throw a stick, and as you see,
It brings back half a tree.

A LONG-DISTANCE RELATIONSHIP

Oh lovely Mary Megaphone,
Whisper in my ear,
Tell me that you love me,
Tell me, tell me, dear.

Oh Mary, Mary, let me hear
Those lovely things you say,
But let me first just go and stand
A hundred yards away.

THE MAN WHO MISSES MONDAY
(The Day That No One Likes . . . Right?)

Hideaway Dan, the Ostrich Man,
Renowned throughout the land,
Plants his head on Sunday night
Deep into the sand.

And rooted there within the ground,
Cut off from sight and sound,
He sleeps away that dreaded day
Till Tuesday comes around.

Oh Hideaway Dan! Oh Hideaway Dan!
You're such a clever man!

HANDSOME PRINCE BUTTERFINGERS SEARCHES FOR CINDERELLA

"Whoever owns the foot that this glass slipper fits,
I will, this very day, promise to wed.
And yes, she'll wear a golden crown upon her head,
And . . . opps . . . aah . . . "

(CRASH!)

"Okay, forget what I said."

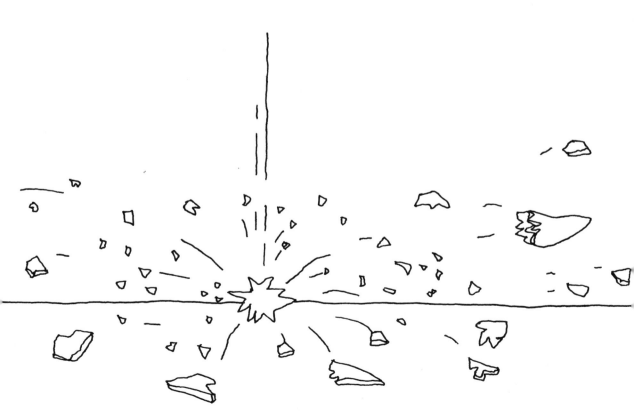

THE CORES OF THE EARTH

The Upside-Down Apple Tree al
Grows downwards through the ground,
Producing lots of apples there—
Rosy, sweet, and round.

But when it's time to dig them up,
The farmer sadly learns,
That though they're red and really ripe,
They're always full of worms!

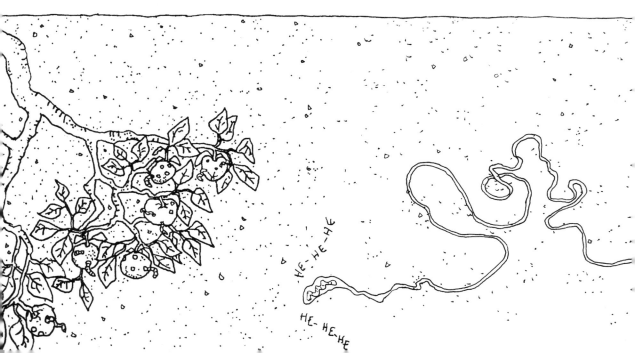

THE WORM THAT HASN'T RETURNED

Haven't you heard?
Somehow Wiggle, my pet worm,
Managed to wriggle off his leash,
And before I could say "You naughty invertebrate beast!"
He was completely out of reach,

Down,

Down,

Down,

Miles underground

Wiggling (and giggling), I'll be bound!

THE FISHERMAN AND
THE MIXED-UP MERMAID

(*A Rather Fishy Tail, I Mean, Tale*)

It was love at first sight
When he hooked Miss Just Right,
A creature—half girl, half fish—
Not something to serve on a dish.

Still, his friends tried to tell him
'Bout mermaids and . . . *tails!*
(The ones all silvery with scales).
But the fisherman, in fact, he paid them no mind,
For love, as you know, is blind!

THE TERRIBLE TOASTER

Tired of toast
And sitting in the kitchen all day,
The toaster ran away,
Thinking in its toaster head,
"There're far better things to toast than bread."
And as it got up and ran along,
It toasted whatever it came upon.

It toasted a dozing doormat,
It toasted the postman's hat.
It toasted a couple of cats, a dog,
Three frogs, a hog, a man on a jog.
Then it toasted his wife, a brand new bike—
In fact, it toasted anything it liked.
It toasted a herd of cows (what a row!),
A flock of sheep, Little Bo Peep,
A field of wheat, passing feet.
It toasted a policeman, an electric fan,
A waving hand, a marching band,
Birds, boys and girls, every word in the world.
A chair, curly hair, underwear. (That made 'em stare!)
A train, a plane, the rain in Spain,
A mountain, a fountain. (Have you given up
    countin'?)
A dozen cars, the twinkling stars, an alien from
    Mars,
The clouds, the breeze, the autumn leaves,
The fish in the seven seas and half the galaxy . . .
And then, would you believe,
That terrible toaster toasted me!
(As you can see.)

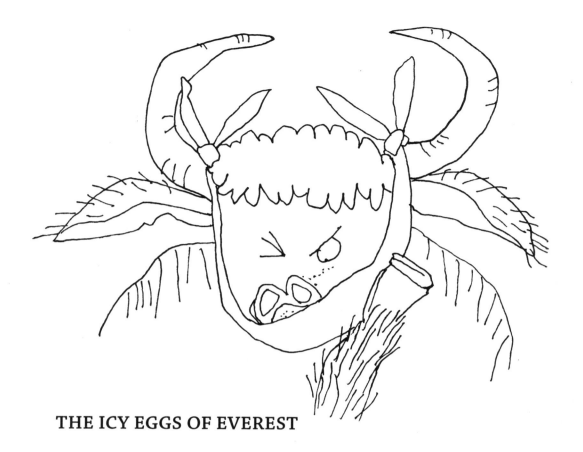

THE ICY EGGS OF EVEREST

The "Himalayers"—those mystic birds
Who live in frosty, wintry worlds—
They lay their eggs, oh, not in nests,
But in the snows of Everest.

And yaks and yetis hunt these eggs,
With icy breath and frozen legs,
So early in the misty morning,
Stumbling 'round and yawning.

And if by chance they find such eggs
They're worth those frozen legs,
They simply can't control their greed
And gulp them down at lightning speed.

But being laid there in the snow
(You might have guessed or rightly know),
The eggs are frozen to the core
And easily break a yeti's jaw.

And . . . that's all I've heard,
Of these peculiar birds.
Except that if, by chance, you meet
A yak or yeti without its teeth,
Or one with say, a broken jaw,
At least you'll think, or know for sure,
Just why it looks so sad, forlorn,
And what it ate for breakfast
At the crack of dawn.

POLE-IN-THE-POND

*(A game kids used to play
before leap-frog was invented)*

Tadpole-vaulting's a dangerous sport,
So make quite sure the pole's not short.
For tadpoles swimming underneath
(The ones with nasty razor teeth)
Like to leap up in the sky
And bite off things there passing by—
The glasses perched upon your nose
And sometimes, half your toes!

WHAT IF

What if the world is an egg that's thrown—
SPLAT—on the wall of the Great Unknown?

What if the world floats up in the air,
A balloon that's heading for a prickly pear?

These are the visions, the terrible themes,
That fill my head, that cloud my dreams.

Strange ideas that come at night
As off I switch the bedroom light.

Still, what if the world is a tennis ball
And the score is forever (and ever) LOVE ALL?

Then surely things will be all right,
And snug in bed I'll sleep tonight.

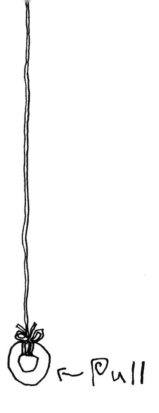

Oh, and while you're here, how about turning off the light?

Remember to press "SWEET" too!

INDEX OF TITLES

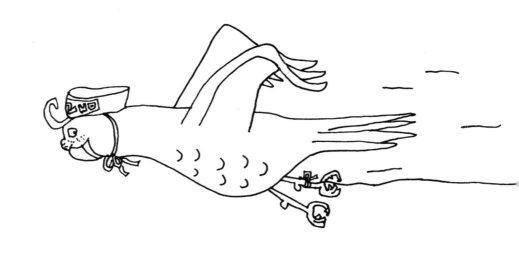

INDEX OF FIRST LINES

Oh, and Mozzmates,

Since you've spied the Holey Whale
And mozzsense, it is yours,
Be the captain of your ship
And sail to further shores.